Scooter fun

By Annette Smith

Tom is at the park.

Ava is at the park.

Mum is at the park.

Look at Tom and Ava.

Tom is going
down the path.

Ava is going

down the path.

Tom is going fast.

Ava is going fast.

Here comes Tom.

Here comes Tom.

Here comes Ava.

Look at Ava!